Companion Press

Workbook

The Psychology of Money

The Financial Guide to Morgan Housel's Principles on Saving, Investing, and Cultivating a Mindset for Lifelong Wealth Building

Companion Press

© 2023 - All Rights Reserved

Workbook: The Psychology of Money

Disclaimer:

This companion workbook is designed to provide educational information on financial advice, techniques, and tips and is based on concepts discussed in The Psychology of Money: Timeless Lessons and Wealth, Greed, and Happiness by [Original Author's Name]. This workbook is an unofficial guide and has not been endorsed or approved by Morgan Housel, the publisher of The Psychology of Money: Timeless Lessons and Wealth, Greed, and Happiness, or any related parties. The information provided in this workbook is for educational and informational purposes only and should not be construed as financial, investment, legal, or other professional advice. The strategies, tips, and techniques discussed in this workbook are not guaranteed to be suitable for all individuals or financial situations. Readers are advised to consult with a qualified financial advisor or other professional before making any significant financial decisions. The author and publisher of this workbook have made every effort to ensure the accuracy and reliability of the information provided, but they do not assume any responsibility for errors, omissions, or contrary interpretations of the subject matter herein. The views and opinions expressed in this workbook are those of the author and do not necessarily reflect the official policy or position of any other agency, organization, employer, or company. Investment in financial markets involves risks, and past performance is not a guarantee of future results. The author and publisher of this workbook are not liable for any loss or damage, including without limitation, indirect or consequential loss or damage, or any loss or damage whatsoever arising from the use of, or reliance on, the information in this workbook. By using this workbook, you agree to take full responsibility for your financial decisions and acknowledge that the author and publisher are not liable for any outcomes resulting from your use of the information provided herein.

Companion Press

Workbook: The Psychology of Money

Table of Contents

Chapter 1: No One's Crazy 6

Chapter 2: Luck & Risk 10

Chapter 3: Never Enough 15

Chapter 4: Cofounding Compounding 19

Chapter 5: Getting Wealthy vs. Staying Wealthy 24

Chapter 6: Tails, You Win 27

Chapter 7: Freedom 33

Chapter 8: Man in the Car Paradox 38

Chapter 9: Wealth is What You Don't See 41

Chapter 10: Save Money 48

Chapter 11: Reasonable > Rational 52

Chapter 12: Surprise 56

Chapter 13: Room for Error 61

Chapter 14: You'll Change 67

Chapter 15: Nothing's Free 71

Chapter 16: You and Me 75

Chapter 17: The Seduction of Pessimism 79

Chapter 18: When You'll Believe Anything 83

Chapter 19: All Together Now 88

Chapter 20: Confessions 92

. Thank you! 97

Companion Press

Chapter 1: No One's Crazy

Chapter 1, "No One's Crazy," is all about understanding why people make the financial choices they do. It's not because they're irrational or don't know better; it's because their choices are shaped by their unique life experiences.

Think of it this way: everyone's financial decisions are like a personal story that's been influenced by their past. For example, John F. Kennedy, who grew up in a wealthy family, didn't feel the sting of the Great Depression like others did. This shaped how he viewed money and risks differently from someone who had to struggle through those tough times.

Similarly, Bill Gross, a big name in investments, made his financial strategies based on the changing interest rates he experienced. His approach was molded by the economic conditions of his era.

The main takeaway from this chapter is simple: when it comes to money, it's not just about how smart you are or what you know. It's hugely influenced by when and where you grew up, and the financial climate of those times. So, when someone's financial decisions seem odd to us, we should try to see the bigger picture of their life story. It's often a mix of personal experiences, how they see the world, and their emotional responses to money.

Companion Press

Key Points

- Financial choices are deeply influenced by individual life experiences and personal history.

- The era and economic climate one grows up in significantly shape their financial perspective and decisions.

- Personal examples: John F. Kennedy's views on money and risk were shaped by his wealthy upbringing during the Great Depression; Bill Gross's investment strategies were influenced by the changing interest rates and economic conditions of his time.

- Understanding financial decisions requires considering a person's background, worldview, and emotional relationship with money.

Mapping Your Financial History and Perspective

This exercise is designed to deepen your understanding of how personal experiences and economic conditions have shaped your financial perspectives and decisions. By reflecting on your life's key events and the economic climate of your formative years, you'll gain insight into the roots of your financial behaviors and choices.

Prepare Your Timeline: Reflect on your life journey, jotting significant events and periods, such as childhood, adolescence, early adulthood, and adulthood. Alongside each period or event, note any notable economic conditions (like recessions, economic booms, or family financial status) and consider how these might have influenced your views on money. Do so below:

CHILDHOOD	ADOLESCENCE	EARLY ADULTHOOD	ADULTHOOD

WRITE ALL EVENTS AND CIRCUMSTANCES WITHIN THEIR RESPECTIVE LIFE PERIOD ABOVE

After completing your timeline, pause to observe the journey you've charted. Notice the ebbs and flows of your financial life, shaped by personal milestones and economic tides. This visual narrative illuminates the roots of your financial mindset. On the next page, you'll find reflective questions crafted to deepen your understanding of this journey.

Reflect on how the environment and experiences of your upbringing shaped your relationship with money. Consider aspects such as your family's financial habits, discussions about money at home, and the values related to wealth imparted by your parents or guardians. How did these early influences mold your current financial beliefs and practices?

Identify a pattern or shift in your financial behavior across different life stages. For example, you may have transitioned from impulse spending to a more strategic savings plan in adulthood. What underlying beliefs or experiences prompted this change?

How has your financial journey contributed to your personal growth? Reflect on the ways it has shaped not just your bank account, but also your character, life decisions, and perspectives. In what ways has it challenged or reinforced your values and priorities?

Workbook: The Psychology of Money

Chapter 2: Luck & Risk

Chapter 2, titled "Luck & Risk," takes us into the often-overlooked world of how chance and danger play into our financial lives. It's a fascinating look at the hidden forces that shape our financial success or failure.

The chapter starts with the story of Bill Gates, pointing out a crucial element of luck in his journey. Gates had early access to a computer, a rare chance that played a big part in his future success. This example sets the stage for the chapter's exploration of how luck and risk, two factors we often don't give enough credit, are central to our financial stories.

The author then explores the concept of risk. It's like a silent factor in our financial decisions, often unnoticed or underestimated. To illustrate this, the chapter talks about lottery tickets. Why do people buy them? It's not always about logic; it's about their life experiences and the unique way they see the world. This extends to bigger financial choices, like investing, where the economic climate of our younger years can heavily influence our approach.

A crucial point the chapter makes is how hard it is to tell luck from skill in financial success. It suggests that for many successful people, luck might have played a bigger role than their skills or decisions. This challenges the common idea that success is all about hard work and smart choices.

Finally, when discussing risk, the chapter warns against overconfidence. Not seeing the role of risk in our financial decisions can lead to big problems, as shown by stories of financial downfalls. It's a reminder that in the world of money, both the winds of chance and the storms of risk are always at play.

Key Points

- Recognize the role of luck in financial success and acknowledge that it often intertwines with skill and hard work.

- Be aware of and account for risk in all financial decisions, understanding that it can be a silent but significant factor.

- Reflect on how personal experiences, particularly those from younger years, shape risk-taking behaviors and investment strategies.

- Challenge the notion that financial success is solely the result of hard work and smart choices, considering the potential impact of chance.

- Guard against overconfidence in financial planning by acknowledging the unpredictability of risk and its possible consequences.

Luck, Risk, and Financial Decision-Making

In Chapter 2, we explored the roles of luck and risk in financial decision-making. To bring these concepts to life, this exercise encourages you to actively apply them to a current financial decision, such as an investment or a career move. Through this hands-on approach, you'll gather relevant information, evaluate luck and risk factors, consult with others, and make an informed choice. The goal is to transform the theoretical insights from the chapter into practical skills, enhancing your understanding and decision-making in real-world financial situations.

Choose a financial decision you're currently facing or considering. This could be an investment opportunity, a major purchase, a career change, or any other significant financial choice. Write about this financial decision below, and why you chose it.

_____

_____

_____

_____

Actively research this decision. Gather relevant information about potential risks and rewards. This could involve reading financial reports, seeking advice from experts, or analyzing market trends.

_____

_____

_____

_____

Now, consider the potential factors that come into play regarding this financial decision. What luck factors might you experience, and why? What risk factors might you experience, and why? Fill in the table below.

Luck Factors	Risk Factors

Weigh the luck and risk factors against each other. How do they balance out? Are the potential rewards worth the risks? Consider alternative options. Are there safer or more advantageous paths?

_____
_____
_____

Workbook: The Psychology of Money

What lessons have you learned from this decision-making process? How can these lessons be applied to future financial decisions?

Companion Press

Chapter 3: Never Enough

Chapter 3, "Enough is Enough," is a real eye-opener about figuring out what 'enough' money looks like for you and why chasing more and more can lead you astray. It kicks off with this intriguing story about Joseph Heller, the famous writer. He's at this glitzy party thrown by a billionaire and has this moment of clarity: he's content with his own wealth, something the mega-rich host can't seem to grasp.

Then, the chapter takes a dramatic turn with the tales of Rajat Gupta and Bernie Madoff, two guys who were swimming in cash but couldn't shake off their thirst for more. Gupta, a high-flying executive, climbed to the top of the corporate ladder but couldn't stop there. His relentless pursuit of more led him down a path of illegal insider trading, ultimately costing him his reputation and freedom. It's a stark reminder of how the never-ending chase for wealth can blur the lines of right and wrong.

Bernie Madoff's story is even more jaw-dropping. Here's a guy who ran the largest Ponzi scheme in history, amassing billions. Despite this, his greed kept pushing him until it all crumbled, leading to a life behind bars. These stories aren't just about the fall of two rich men; they're cautionary tales about what can happen when 'enough' is never enough.

The chapter doesn't just leave you with these dramatic stories. It dives into why we sometimes can't feel satisfied with what we have. It's about how we look at others and think we need to match up, and how society's flashy standards can make us want more than is actually necessary.

Wrapping up, the chapter brings it home by emphasizing how important it is to find your own balance. What does 'enough' mean to you?.

Key Points

- Enough' money is subjective; recognizing personal limits is essential for contentment.

- Relentless pursuit of wealth can lead to unethical behavior and serious consequences, as shown in the stories of Rajat Gupta and Bernie Madoff.

- Societal and psychological pressures often drive the desire for more wealth, leading to dissatisfaction.

- Identifying a personal definition of 'enough' is key to financial well-being.

Defining Your "Enough"

Reflect on your own life and finances. What does 'enough' mean to you? Consider your goals, values, and what truly makes you happy.

_____
_____
_____
_____
_____
_____
_____
_____

Write down a list of things that you consider essential for a contented and fulfilling life. How does this list align with your current financial goals and spending habits?

_____
_____
_____
_____
_____
_____
_____
_____

Have you reached your 'enough' yet? How can you tell, and what changes or decisions might you need to make to align your current financial situation with your personal definition of 'enough'? Reflect on the steps you can take to bridge any gaps between where you are now and where you want to be in terms of financial contentment and life fulfillment.

_____
_____
_____
_____

After identifying gaps between their current situation and their 'enough', create a step-by-step action plan to address these gaps.

Goals (How can you get there if you aren't already? This could be paying off debt, investing, developing side hustles, or more.)

_____
_____
_____
_____

Lifestyle (How can you adjust your lifestyle? This could involve cutting expenses.)

_____
_____
_____
_____

Companion Press

Chapter 4: Cofounding Compounding

Chapter 4, "Confounding Compounding," unpacks the incredible force of compounding and how it can transform finances over time, much like subtle changes lead to ice ages. This chapter uses this natural phenomenon as a metaphor to illustrate the gradual yet powerful effect of compounding in financial growth.

Central to this chapter is the story of Warren Buffett, a name synonymous with extraordinary wealth. But it's not just his smart investment choices that made him rich; it's also about when he started and how long he's been at it. Buffett began investing as a teenager and kept at it for over seven decades. This long-term involvement allowed him to harness the full potential of compounding, turning modest gains into a massive fortune over time. His story is a vivid example of the chapter's key message: the true magic of compounding works best over extended periods.

The chapter explores why compounding is often misunderstood or underestimated. It explains that small, steady growth, compounded over many years, can lead to astonishingly large sums. This idea can seem almost unbelievable compared to the common belief that rapid, high returns are the best way to build wealth. However, the latter approach often involves higher risks and can lead to significant losses.

Understanding the power of compounding is crucial for long-term financial success, the author emphasizes. It's about seeing the big picture: wealth can grow exponentially if you let your investments do their work overtime. This means adopting a mindset of patience and focusing on long-term goals, rather than getting caught up in the pursuit of quick gains.

Key Points

- Compounding is a powerful force in financial growth, working best over long periods.

- Warren Buffett's wealth is largely due to his early start in investing and the long duration of his investments, exemplifying the power of compounding.

- Compounding is often misunderstood; steady, small growth over many years can result in large sums.

- Long-term financial success hinges on understanding and utilizing the power of compounding, favoring patience and long-term goals over quick gains.

Companion Press

Crafting Your Compounding Plan

In Chapter 4, "Confounding Compounding," we explored the transformative power of compounding in finance. To apply these concepts practically, this workbook exercise guides you through creating your own compounding plan. This plan is a strategic approach to grow your wealth over time, utilizing the principles of compounding interest.

Identify one long-term financial goal. This could be a retirement fund, buying a house, or any significant future expense. Write this financial goal below, along with your "why" it is important to you.

My current long-term financial goal is [_____]

This is important to me because…

_____

_____

_____

_____

Based on your current budget and expenses, decide how much you can realistically invest each month. Remember, consistency is key. Even small, regular investments can grow significantly over time due to the power of compounding interest.

$ _____

Detail your investment plan. Where will you be putting your monthly savings? Consider different options like high-interest savings accounts, index funds, IRAs, etc., based on your risk tolerance and goal timeline.

Investment Option	Reasoning	Goal Alignment (1-10)

Given the research you've done, which investment opportunity makes the most sense for your goals? Pick up to three of your favorite options, and outline why below.

_____
_____
_____
_____
_____

Companion Press

Extra Expert Tips for Your Compounding Plan

To maximize the benefits of compounding interest, it's essential to choose the right financial tools and accounts. This section will guide you through some of the best options currently available, from high-yield savings accounts to innovative investment apps and certificates of deposit. Each of these options offers unique advantages to suit different saving and investment styles. By understanding these choices, you can better tailor your compounding plan to your financial goals and preferences.

High-Yield Savings Accounts:
High-yield savings accounts are a great starting point for compounding interest. NerdWallet lists several banks offering competitive annual percentage yields (APYs). For instance, American Express offers a 4.30% APY, and Barclays provides a 4.35% APY, with no minimum to open the account. Bask Bank and BMO Alto offer even higher rates at 5.10% APY, and Bread Savings tops the list with a 5.15% APY, albeit with a $100 minimum to open the account.

Investment Apps:
- Acorns offers the added benefit of earning cash back on purchases, which can then be invested. It's particularly suited for those willing to take a bit of risk for potentially higher returns.
- Qapital offers a unique approach to saving by linking actions (like hitting your daily step goal) to saving a certain amount. It turns saving into a fun and almost addictive game.
- Twine is another app worth considering, especially for couples looking to save together towards a common goal.
- Varo is a mobile banking app offering a substantial 5.00% APY on balances up to $5,000, which is significantly higher than the average savings account.

Chapter 5: Getting Wealthy vs. Staying Wealthy

Chapter 5, "Getting Wealthy vs. Staying Wealthy," opens with an engaging story comparing two very different experiences during the 1929 stock market crash. Jesse Livermore, a famed stock trader known for his risk-taking, stands in contrast to Abraham Germansky, an ordinary investor. This comparison sets the scene for the chapter's deeper exploration into the distinct skills required for accumulating wealth versus preserving it.

The key theme of the chapter is the stark difference between the strategies needed to get rich and those required to stay rich. To accumulate wealth, taking bold risks, being optimistic, and seizing opportunities are often necessary. It's like being in a race where speed and agility count. But to maintain that wealth, the approach changes dramatically. Here, caution, humility, and a keen awareness of how luck might have played a role in past successes are crucial. It's more like a marathon, where endurance and pacing are key to lasting success.

The chapter then dives into the unique skill sets needed for each phase. Making money is one thing, but holding onto it is a completely different ball game. Warren Buffett's journey is a perfect example of someone who mastered both. He not only made savvy investment choices but also knew how to preserve and grow his wealth over time. On the flip side, the chapter also brings up stories of individuals who initially saw great financial success but couldn't sustain it, illustrating the pitfalls of focusing solely on wealth accumulation without a strategy for retention.

Another interesting concept the chapter introduces is "tail events." These are rare but significant occurrences that can have a huge impact on financial outcomes. In industries like venture capital and technology, a few successful investments can massively outweigh numerous failures.

Key Points

- Getting rich often involves risk-taking and seizing opportunities, while staying rich requires caution and humility.

- Long-term endurance is more crucial than achieving short-term, high returns in wealth management.

- Different skills are needed for accumulating wealth versus preserving it.

- Examples like Warren Buffett show the importance of both making and keeping money.

- "Tail events" demonstrate that rare but significant decisions can greatly impact financial outcomes.

- The key to wealth is not just earning it, but also consistently maintaining and growing it.

- Financial planning should balance the pursuit of growth with the awareness of risks.

- A long-term perspective is essential in both acquiring and retaining wealth.

Risk Management and Wealth Preservation Plan

This activity is designed to enhance your understanding of risk management as a key component of wealth preservation. By evaluating your current financial strategies and creating a comprehensive risk management plan, you will develop skills crucial for maintaining and safeguarding your wealth.

Assess Your Current Financial Risk: Begin by assessing the current level of risk in your financial portfolio.	
Identify Potential Risks: List potential financial risks you might face, such as market downturns, job loss, or unexpected expenses.	
Develop a Risk Mitigation Plan: For each identified risk, develop a strategy to mitigate it. This might include diversifying investments, setting up an emergency fund, obtaining insurance, or adjusting your retirement plan.	
Wealth Preservation Goals: Set specific goals related to preserving your wealth. These goals should focus on maintaining and safeguarding your assets rather than on aggressive growth.	

Chapter 6: Tails, You Win

Chapter 6, "Tails, You Win," brings to light a fascinating aspect of financial success: the outsized impact of rare but significant decisions. The chapter begins with the story of Warren Buffett, a renowned investor whose extraordinary wealth largely stems from a few key investments, coupled with the long-term growth of these investments. This narrative sets the stage for the chapter's exploration of 'tail events' in finance, those few pivotal moments that can drastically shape one's financial future.

The chapter emphasizes that achieving success in investing isn't about consistently making good decisions. Instead, it's about those few remarkable choices that stand out. These 'tail events' are infrequent but crucial in determining overall financial success. The chapter makes it clear that these moments, while rare, have the potential to dramatically alter an investor's trajectory.

Another important focus of the chapter is on the concept of endurance in investing. It's not just about scoring big wins; it's equally about avoiding significant losses. Staying the course through market fluctuations is vital to allow the benefits of your investments, and the rare big wins, to fully manifest. The idea is to be consistent and patient, giving your investments time to grow and capitalize on these key moments.

The author also addresses a common mistake in investment strategies: the overemphasis on consistently picking winners. The reality, as the chapter explains, is that maintaining a steady approach, even with some investments not panning out, can lead to significant long-term gains. This is because a few successful investments can compensate for less successful ones, thanks to the compound effect of these rare but successful choices.

In conclusion, Chapter 6 imparts a key lesson on financial strategy: the importance of recognizing and preparing for these 'tail events.' It's about understanding that sometimes a few big, successful decisions can have a more profound impact than many smaller ones. The chapter advocates for a long-term approach to investing, emphasizing the need for patience and stability to see substantial growth in wealth.

Key Points

- Learn from Warren Buffett's approach by focusing on high-quality investments and holding them for the long term.

- Recognize the impact of 'tail events' where a small number of significant decisions can greatly influence overall financial success.

- Emphasize endurance over constant wins by staying invested and consistent rather than trying to win with every investment.

- Avoid major financial losses to protect your wealth as much as growing it.

- Be patient with your investments, giving them time to mature and capitalize on growth potential.

- Don't over-focus on picking winners, understanding that a few successful investments can offset less successful ones.

- Prepare for rare, impactful financial opportunities by staying informed and ready to capitalize on these moments.

- Adopt a long-term perspective, focusing on steady, long-term growth rather than short-term gains.

- Balance risk and reward by being mindful of risks while seeking opportunities for substantial growth.

Tail Event Strategy Development

Understanding and preparing for 'tail events' – rare but impactful occurrences – is crucial for anyone looking to navigate the financial market successfully. These events can dramatically shape your financial journey, making it essential to develop a strategy that not only identifies potential tail events but also aligns with your risk tolerance and financial goals. This exercise aims to enhance your skills in recognizing, strategizing, and managing investments related to these significant events, ultimately contributing to a more robust and informed approach to your financial planning.

Identify Potential Tail Events:
Think about potential 'tail events' in your current investment environment. These could be emerging technologies, market shifts, or new business opportunities. List at least three potential 'tail events' and describe why you think they have the potential for substantial impact. (Think Artificial Intelligence, Semiconductors, etc.)

_____

_____

_____

_____

Assess Your Current Portfolio:
Evaluate your current investment portfolio. Are there investments that could potentially become 'tail events'?

_____

_____

_____

_____

Develop a Tail Event Strategy:
Based on your findings, develop a strategy to incorporate potential 'tail events' into your investment plan. This may involve allocating a portion of your portfolio to higher-risk, high-reward investments or setting aside funds to capitalize on emerging opportunities. Outline your tailored 'tail event' strategy, including specific actions and allocation plans.

_____

_____

_____

_____

Risk Management Plan:
Consider the risks associated with pursuing 'tail events' and develop a plan to manage these risks. This might include setting loss limits or conducting regular portfolio reviews. Create a risk management plan for your 'tail event' strategy.

_____

_____

_____

_____

Monitoring and Adjustment:
Establish a routine for monitoring the market and your investments for signs of potential 'tail events'. Plan for regular reviews of your strategy to make adjustments as needed. Set up a schedule for monitoring and review, and detail how you will adjust your strategy based on market changes.

An Insightful Tip About 2024 Tail Events

Heading into 2024, the remarkable progress in artificial intelligence (AI) is shaping up to be a significant trend. This advancement in AI is expected to bring about a wave of efficiency and innovation, opening new paths for business growth and profitability. Specifically, its transformative impact will be felt in healthcare, enhancing diagnostic and treatment capabilities, and in banking, where smoother operations and improved customer service are anticipated. Beyond these sectors, AI's contribution to environmental efforts is noteworthy, especially in optimizing energy usage and aiding in climate change initiatives.

Here's a more detailed look:

AI's Global Impact: Comparable to the internet's revolutionary influence, AI is poised to significantly alter business practices and the economic landscape, potentially ushering in fresh financial opportunities.

Real-World AI Implementation: The transition from theoretical AI discussions to real-world applications is increasingly evident. Opportunities for investment are emerging, particularly in areas like semiconductor manufacturing and technological innovation.

Investing in AI for the Long Haul: AI's expansion into crucial sectors such as healthcare and environmental technology is in sync with a strategy of long-term investment. This approach involves identifying and leveraging significant, occasional opportunities that promise substantial returns over extended periods.

For investors, understanding and adapting to these developments in AI is essential for identifying potential areas of growth and aligning investment strategies with the evolving technological landscape.

Companion Press

Chapter 7: Freedom

Chapter 7, titled "Freedom," explores the idea that true wealth is less about financial figures and more about the freedom and control it gives you in life. The chapter starts with a thought-provoking idea: the greatest wealth is being able to wake up and decide what you want to do each day. This concept moves away from traditional views of wealth, focusing instead on the autonomy and choices that financial stability can bring.

This chapter discusses how financial wealth links to happiness. It points out that while happiness means different things to different people, having control over your life is often a key part of it. Here, money is seen as more than just a way to buy things; it's a tool for controlling your time and making your own choices.

A large part of the chapter looks at the psychological side of wealth. It suggests that being in control of your life can make you happier than just having money or things. This leads to the idea that the best thing money can do is give you control over your time, which can lead to independence and making your own choices.

The chapter also talks about the trap of comparing your wealth to others and the pressure to show off what you have. It points out that real wealth is often the money you haven't spent – the things you didn't buy, the upgrades you passed on. In other words, true wealth is in the financial resources that give you choices and freedom, not just in the things you can show.

In the end, Chapter 7 changes how we think about wealth. It suggests looking at wealth to get more time and control in your life, not just as a way to get more things. The chapter says the real value of wealth is in the freedom and options it gives you, which can make a big difference in your happiness and life quality.

Key Points

- View wealth as a means to gain control over your life, not just as a way to accumulate things.

- Recognize that the greatest wealth is having the freedom to choose how to spend your time each day.

- Understand that happiness often comes from having control over your life, which financial stability can provide.

- Use money as a tool for gaining independence and making your own choices, rather than solely for purchasing goods.

- Avoid the trap of comparing your wealth to others, as true wealth is often in unspent money and the choices it offers.

- Focus on building wealth that gives you options and freedom, rather than just material possessions.

- Reevaluate your financial goals to prioritize personal freedom and autonomy, aligning them with what truly makes you happy.

Companion Press

Financial Freedom Exercise

While wealth is often viewed in terms of numbers, this exercise shifts the focus to the freedom and control that wealth can provide. By reflecting on your personal definition of wealth, assessing your current financial situation, and realigning your goals, you will develop a more meaningful and fulfilling approach to managing your finances. This process is not just about increasing your bank balance; it's about enhancing the quality of your life by using your resources to gain more freedom and happiness.

Personal Definition of Wealth:
Reflect on what wealth means to you beyond financial figures. How does it relate to your personal freedom and happiness? Write a short paragraph on your definition of wealth and how it contributes to your sense of freedom and happiness.

_____

_____

_____

_____

_____

_____

_____

_____

_____

_____

Current Financial Assessment:

Evaluate your current financial status. How much of your wealth is currently contributing to your freedom and control over your life? List your main income sources, savings, and investments. Note which aspects contribute to your sense of freedom and which do not.

Income Sources	Savings Accounts	Investments

Financial Goal Reassessment:

Revisit your financial goals in light of your new understanding of wealth as a tool for freedom. Are your goals aligned with achieving more control over your life? Redefine your financial goals to emphasize personal freedom and control. This might involve changing savings targets, investment strategies, or spending habits.

_____

_____

_____

_____

_____

_____

_____

Action Plan for Financial Independence:

Based on your reassessment, create a practical action plan to use your finances to increase your personal freedom. Outline specific steps you will take to adjust your finances to align with your new goals. This could include budget adjustments, new savings plans, or investment in skills/education that offer greater independence.

Steps to Accomplish Your New Financial Goals
1.
2.
3.
4.
5.
6.
7.

Workbook: The Psychology of Money

Chapter 8: Man in the Car Paradox

Chapter 8, "The Man in the Car Paradox", examines the way we often misjudge wealth. Housel questions the usual signs of wealth, like owning fancy cars or luxury items. He points out that these things show how much someone spends, not how much they actually have. The paradox is this: seeing someone with a pricey car makes us think they're rich, but real wealth is about the money you save and invest, not the flashy things you buy.

Housel explains that spending money to show off leads to having less money. He talks about the idea of "enough," highlighting the importance of knowing when you're financially satisfied. Understanding this can help you save and invest better, instead of wasting money on things just to impress others.

The chapter also looks at why we spend so much. Often, it's because of social pressure or trying to keep up with others. Housel suggests that we should focus more on being financially stable and independent, instead of trying to look wealthy.

In "The Man in the Car Paradox," Housel encourages us to rethink what real wealth means. He advises moving away from buying things to show off wealth, and towards saving and investing for the future. He makes a strong case for invisible wealth - the money you haven't spent - as the real sign of financial success.

Companion Press

Key Points

- Wealth is often misjudged by visible luxury items, which reflect spending, not actual wealth.

- True wealth lies in unspent and invested money, not in expensive purchases.

- Spending to show off often leads to having less money in the long run.

- Understanding the concept of "enough" is key to financial satisfaction and smarter saving and investing.

- Social pressure and the desire to keep up with others can lead to unnecessary spending.

- Real financial stability comes from independence, not from appearing wealthy.

- Rethinking wealth means focusing on saving and investing for the future, rather than displaying it.

- Invisible wealth, or unspent money, is the true indicator of financial success.

Workbook: The Psychology of Money

My Status Symbol

Instructions: Reflect on a purchase you made primarily for status or frivolous desire. It could be a car, gadget, clothing, or any item. Answer the following questions in the space provided:
What motivated this purchase?
How did it make you feel initially, and how do you feel about it now?
Did it affect how others perceived you? How?
Would you make a similar purchase again? Why or why not?

Companion Press

Chapter 9: Wealth is What You Don't See

Chapter 9, "Wealth is What You Don't See", takes a deeper look at what real wealth means. Housel explains that true wealth isn't about showing off with expensive things. Instead, it's about the money you haven't spent. This means your savings and investments, the things you own that don't necessarily show up in your lifestyle.

Housel says real wealth is about having financial assets that you haven't turned into stuff you can show off. It's more about having choices, freedom, and a safety net for when things get tough. He points out that just because someone doesn't look rich doesn't mean they aren't. Real wealth is often invisible – it's in the money you save and the financial security you build, not in the fancy things you buy.

The chapter talks about how society often makes us feel like we need to show our wealth. This can lead to a problem where, as you earn more, you also spend more, a habit known as 'lifestyle creep.' But spending more as you earn more can actually stop you from building real wealth.

Housel emphasizes the importance of how much you save, not just how much you earn. He explains that having a high saving rate is a better sign of wealth than just having a high income. It's not just about the money coming in, but also how much of it you manage to keep.

The chapter ends by saying that financial independence and security are more important than having lots of things. Housel advises focusing on saving and planning for the future, rather than just buying things to show off. He encourages readers to build wealth that lasts and gives them real freedom, instead of getting caught up in buying things to look wealthy.

Key Points

- True wealth isn't shown through expensive items but lies in unspent money, savings, and investments.

- Real wealth means having financial assets not converted into visible luxury items.

- Wealth provides choices, freedom, and a safety net, rather than just material possessions.

- Outward appearances of wealth can be misleading; real wealth is often invisible.

- Society pressures individuals to display wealth, leading to 'lifestyle creep' where expenses rise with income.

- Building wealth is more about saving effectively than just earning a high income.

- A high saving rate is a more accurate indicator of wealth than a high income.

- Financial independence and security should be prioritized over materialistic displays.

- Focusing on long-term wealth accumulation is more beneficial than succumbing to consumerism.

Building My Invisible Wealth Exercise

This exercise aims to guide you in setting and understanding the importance of savings goals over various time frames. By writing about these goals, you'll gain insight into how they contribute to your invisible wealth, enhancing your financial stability and freedom.

Short-term Savings Goal (1 year):
Reflect on your current financial situation and set a realistic savings goal for the next year. Write a detailed description of your one-year goal, including the specific amount you aim to save and what this goal represents for your invisible wealth. Explain why this goal is important to you.

1-Year Goal	Amount to Save

This goal is extremely important for me to accomplish because…

_____

_____

_____

_____

_____

_____

Medium-term Savings Goal (5 years):

Think about where you want to be financially in five years. Set a savings goal that aligns with your broader financial aspirations. Describe your five-year savings goal in detail. Explain how achieving this goal will contribute to your financial independence or other long-term aspirations.

5-Year Goal	Amount to Save

This goal is extremely important for me to accomplish because…

Long-term Savings Goal (10 years):

Consider your long-term financial security and freedom. Set a goal that reflects your vision of financial stability a decade from now. Write about your ten-year financial goal, detailing what this goal represents in terms of your life's larger financial picture. Discuss the impact this goal will have on your personal and financial freedom.

10-Year Goal	Amount to Save

This goal is extremely important for me to accomplish because…

Reflection on Invisible Wealth:

Reflect on how achieving these goals contributes to building your invisible wealth. For each goal, write a reflection on how reaching this milestone will enhance your financial security, freedom, and overall well-being. Consider the choices and opportunities each goal will unlock.

Short/Med/Long Milestone	Reflection

Action Steps:

Based on your goals, identify specific steps to achieve them. This could include creating a budget, finding ways to reduce expenses, or exploring additional income sources. Under each goal, list the actions you will take to reach these milestones. Be as specific as possible about the steps you'll take and how they will help you achieve your savings goals.

Short/Med/Long Goal	*Action*

Through this exercise, you'll not only set clear savings goals but also understand their significance in terms of your overall financial health. Writing about these goals encourages a deeper connection with them, fostering a mindset geared towards long-term financial success and independence.

Chapter 10: Save Money

Chapter 10, titled "Save Money," focuses on the crucial role of saving in achieving financial well-being. Morgan Housel explains that saving money is about more than just building wealth; it's key to gaining freedom and flexibility in life.

Housel begins by tackling a common myth: that you need a high income to save effectively. He argues that saving is more about your mindset and habits with money than how much you earn. Even those with modest incomes can build up significant savings over time if they save consistently and with discipline.

A major point Housel makes is about the power of compounding. He shows that even small amounts saved regularly can grow into a large sum over the years. This means that a modest saving rate can lead to big financial growth if you give it enough time.

The chapter also looks at why saving can be hard. Housel points out that we're often tempted to spend because of consumerism and pressure to keep up with others. He suggests creating a personal saving philosophy that matches your long-term financial goals and values, instead of being influenced by what others are doing.

Housel highlights the importance of having a financial safety net. He explains that savings can protect you against unexpected life events like job loss or health issues. This safety net isn't just about money; it also gives you peace of mind, knowing you're prepared for life's uncertainties.

Key Points

- Saving is crucial for financial well-being and provides freedom and flexibility, not just wealth accumulation.

- Effective saving depends more on mindset and habits than on earning a high income.

- Consistent and disciplined saving can lead to significant savings over time, even with a modest income.

- The power of compounding turns small, regular savings into substantial wealth over the long term.

- Saving can be challenging due to consumerism and societal pressure to spend.

- Develop a personal saving philosophy that aligns with your long-term financial goals and values.

- Savings act as a financial safety net, offering protection against life's uncertainties like job loss or health issues.

- A financial safety net provides peace of mind and prepares you for unexpected events.

Workbook: The Psychology of Money

30-Day Savings Boost

Over the next 30 days, you'll incrementally increase your savings in a manageable yet impactful way. This exercise is not just about setting aside money; it's an exploration into the discipline of saving and the satisfaction of watching your financial assets grow day by day. Make it a point to save some amount, any amount, of money each day in a 30 day period.

1	2	3	4	5
6	7	8	9	10
11	12	13	14	15
16	17	18	19	20
21	22	23	24	25
26	27	28	29	30

After you complete the 30-day savings challenge, answer the questions below:

How did this exercise change your daily spending habits? Did you find yourself making different choices to ensure you saved each day?

_____

_____

_____

Were you surprised by the total amount saved at the end of 30 days? How does this reinforce the concept of small savings accumulating over time?

_____

_____

_____

Has your mindset towards money and saving changed as a result of this exercise? In what ways?

_____

_____

_____

_____

_____

_____

Chapter 11: Reasonable > Rational

Chapter 11, "Reasonable > Rational", discusses the difference between being rational and being reasonable in financial decisions. Housel explains that while making rational, data-based decisions is often seen as ideal, being reasonable – which means making decisions that are practical and fit your own life – can be more beneficial.

Housel starts by explaining the difference between rational and reasonable actions. Rational actions are based purely on logic and data, but reasonable actions consider personal feelings and individual situations. He points out that focusing too much on rationality in finance can lead to choices that might be technically right but not the best for your unique circumstances.

The chapter looks at how personal experiences and emotions play a big role in how we handle money. Housel notes that everyone's approach to money is shaped by their own life experiences, so what's rational on paper might not fit everyone's reality.

Housel then talks about how personal finance is more about the person than the finances. He says that since everyone's life is different, there's no one-size-fits-all financial advice. He advises readers to think about their own values, goals, and life story when making financial choices.

Overall, Housel suggests that in personal finance, being reasonable – making decisions that make sense for your own life and feelings – is often more important than just doing what's logically rational.

Companion Press

Key Points

- Rational decisions are based on logic and data; reasonable decisions consider personal context and emotions.

- Personal feelings and unique life situations are crucial in making financial choices.

- Personal finance is highly individual, shaped by each person's experiences and values.

- Reasonable financial choices, aligned with personal situations, often outweigh strictly rational decisions.

Workbook: The Psychology of Money

Personal Decision Analysis

This exercise helps you explore how personal emotions, experiences, and values influence your financial choices. By analyzing your recent financial decisions from both rational and reasonable perspectives, you gain insight into how well these choices align with your personal context. This reflection is vital for developing a more holistic, satisfying approach to managing your finances, moving beyond purely data-driven choices to make decisions that truly fit your life. After you fill in the table, move on to the next page to complete the reflection questions. Reminder: Rational aspects are those based on logical analysis and objective data. Reasonable aspects are those that take into account your personal feelings, experiences, and unique life circumstances.

Decision	*Rational Aspects*	*Reasonable Aspects*

The following reflection questions will guide you through this introspection, helping you to connect your rational and reasonable decision-making aspects with your overall financial well-being.

How well did you balance rational and reasonable aspects in your financial decisions? Which aspect dominated more and why?

_____
_____
_____
_____

What emotions played a key role in your reasonable decision-making? How did these emotions align or conflict with the rational data?

_____
_____
_____
_____

Reflect on your satisfaction level with each decision. Did the decisions that leaned more on reasonableness bring more contentment?

_____
_____
_____
_____

Chapter 12: Surprise

Chapter 12, "Surprise," explores the unpredictable nature of financial markets and personal finance. Housel emphasizes planning for the unexpected rather than precisely forecasting the future. He explores the limitations of financial predictions, noting most models fail to account for real-world randomness. Historical events like the 2008 crisis illustrate the impact of unforeseen financial occurrences.

Shifting to personal finance, Housel explains how surprise expenses or life changes can significantly impact financial health. He advocates for building a margin of safety, such as an emergency fund, to buffer against unforeseen events and reduce stress.

The chapter also addresses psychological aspects of financial surprises. Housel notes people often overreact, either taking excessive risks in good times or becoming overly cautious in bad times. He recommends maintaining a balanced perspective to avoid extreme reactions.

In conclusion, "Surprise" highlights the importance of resilience and adaptability in financial planning, emphasizing preparedness over prediction. This approach encourages accepting uncertainty and building robust financial strategies.

Companion Press

Key Points

- Financial markets and personal finance are inherently unpredictable.

- Planning for the unexpected is more effective than precise forecasting.

- Financial models often fail to account for real-world randomness.

- Historical events, like the 2008 crisis, demonstrate the impact of unforeseen financial changes.

- Surprise expenses can significantly affect personal financial health.

- Building a financial safety net, such as an emergency fund, is crucial.

- People may overreact to financial surprises, either by taking excessive risks or being overly cautious. Maintaining a balanced perspective is advised to manage these reactions.

- Emphasizes the importance of resilience, adaptability, and preparedness in financial planning.

Workbook: The Psychology of Money

Financial Surprise Preparedness Plan

Creating a financial surprise preparedness plan is a crucial exercise in managing personal finances effectively. It helps you anticipate unexpected events, assess your current financial readiness, and strategize to improve resilience. This plan also encourages examining your emotional reactions to surprises, guiding you to maintain balance and adaptability in financial matters.

Identify Potential Surprises:

List possible unexpected financial events, both positive and negative, that could occur in your life. This step helps in anticipating a range of scenarios, from sudden expenses like a car breakdown or medical emergency to positive surprises such as receiving a bonus or inheritance. Write some of the most likely potential events down below.

Negative Surprises	Positive Surprises	Why Is It Likely?

To create a safety net plan, start by determining how much you need in your emergency fund, usually 3-6 months' worth of expenses. Then, develop a savings strategy to build this fund. This could involve setting a fixed percentage of your income aside each month, automating transfers to a savings account, or finding ways to reduce expenses and channel the savings into your fund. Detail what is most logical for your personal safety net below.

I will save [   ] every month to build a financial safety net.

I will build this safety net by [   ]

Building this safety net is important to me because…

You've taken an important step by outlining potential financial surprises and starting to create a plan for building your safety net. This plan is crucial for enhancing your financial security and ensuring peace of mind. Remember to periodically review and adjust your list of potential surprises, as circumstances in life can change, requiring updates to your plan. Stay committed to your savings strategy; consistency is key to successfully building your emergency fund. Even small, regular contributions can grow into a significant safety net over time.

Extra Tips for Building a Safety Net

In building a comprehensive financial safety net, incorporating various strategies is essential. This section outlines key components, including insurance integration, tailored plans for married couples, effective methods for building and preserving emergency funds, and the importance of proper usage of these funds that experts recommend. Each aspect plays a vital role in ensuring financial security and independence, helping you navigate through unforeseen financial challenges.

Insurance Integration: Include life insurance and disability insurance as core components of your financial safety net. Life insurance provides security for your family in case of your death, while disability insurance protects your income in case of inability to work due to illness or injury.

Married Couples' Safety Nets: It's advisable for married couples to maintain separate emergency funds. This approach offers financial security in case of relationship changes, ensuring individual financial independence.

Building and Preserving Emergency Funds: Consistently setting aside a portion of your income is crucial. The 50/30/20 rule, where 20% of income goes to savings, is an effective model. To protect your savings, consider high-yield savings accounts and automate your savings to make the process effortless and consistent.

Consequences of Misusing Emergency Funds: Using emergency funds for non-emergency purposes, like vacations, can leave you financially vulnerable when real emergencies occur. It's important to strictly reserve these funds for unforeseen circumstances.

Chapter 13: Room for Error

Chapter 13 "Room for Error", explores the critical concept of incorporating margins of safety in financial decision-making. This chapter underscores the inevitability of errors and the unpredictable nature of life and financial markets, highlighting the necessity of preparing for less-than-ideal scenarios.

Housel begins by stressing that no matter how confident we are in our financial plans or predictions, there is always a possibility of error due to unforeseen events or miscalculations. He emphasizes that these errors are not just possible but are, in fact, inevitable. The key message here is not to avoid errors – which is impossible – but to plan for them by building room for error into our financial strategies.

A significant part of the chapter is dedicated to illustrating how a margin of safety can act as a buffer against these inevitable mistakes. Housel uses practical examples, such as investing with a cushion that can absorb unexpected market downturns, or saving more than you think you'll need for retirement. These examples demonstrate how planning for more than the minimum requirements can provide a safety net, reducing stress and potential financial harm when things don't go as planned.

Housel explores the psychological comfort that comes with having a margin of safety. Knowing that you have a buffer can make you more confident in your financial decisions and more resilient in the face of market volatility or personal financial disruptions.

"Room for Error" presents a compelling argument for the inclusion of safety margins in financial planning. By acknowledging the unpredictable nature of life and the certainty of mistakes, Housel encourages readers to adopt a more cautious and prepared approach to their financial decisions, ultimately aiming for a strategy that is robust enough to withstand the surprises that life invariably throws our way.

Key Points

- Chapter 13 emphasizes the importance of including safety margins in financial plans.

- It highlights that errors and unpredictability are inevitable in finance.

- The chapter advises planning for potential errors, rather than trying to avoid them.

- It illustrates using safety margins, like extra savings or investment cushions, as a buffer against mistakes.

- The chapter underscores the psychological comfort provided by having a financial safety net.

- Housel encourages a cautious and prepared approach to financial decisions.

- The chapter underlines the need for prudence and foresight in personal finance.

Companion Press

Diversifying Your Investments

Diversification is a crucial strategy for managing investment risk. This approach involves spreading your investments across a range of asset classes, industries, and geographic regions. By doing so, you reduce the impact of market volatility. A well-diversified portfolio is less likely to experience significant losses when a particular investment underperforms.

The objective of this exercise is to assist you in creating a diversified portfolio that can better withstand market downturns. This strategy helps avoid concentrating all your investment risk in one area.

How to Diversify a Portfolio:
Balance Across Asset Classes:
Aim for a mix of stocks, bonds, and possibly other assets like real estate or commodities. For instance, if your portfolio is heavily stock-based, consider adding bonds or bond funds to balance it out.

Diversity in Industry and Sector:
Ensure your stock investments are spread across different sectors (technology, healthcare, consumer goods, etc.). Avoid overconcentration in one industry which can be risky if that sector faces downturns.

Geographical Diversification:
Mix domestic and international investments to reduce exposure to a single country's economic fluctuations. Consider international mutual funds or ETFs as an easy way to gain global exposure.

Risk Tolerance Alignment:

Balance riskier investments (like small-cap stocks or emerging markets) with more stable ones (like blue-chip stocks or government bonds). Adjust the mix based on your risk tolerance and investment time horizon. Younger investors might lean more towards growth-oriented investments, while those nearer to retirement may prefer stability.

Short-term vs. Long-term Goals:
Diversify based on your investment goals. Short-term goals may require safer, more liquid assets, while long-term goals can handle more volatility for higher growth potential.

Regular Portfolio Rebalancing:
Revisit your portfolio periodically to ensure it remains aligned with your diversification strategy. Market movements can shift your intended asset allocation over time.

Assessment of Current Portfolio

List your current investments in the table below. Categorize them by asset class, industry, and region. This will help you see where you might be over-concentrated.

Investment Name (Apple, Uber, Etc.)	Asset Class (Bond, Stock, ETF, Etc.)	Industry (Technology, Healthcare, Etc.)	Region (N. America, Europe, Etc.)	Percentage of Your Portfolio

After filling out the "Assessment of Current Portfolio" table, answer the following questions to reflect on your investment concentrations and plan for better diversification:

What patterns do you observe in your portfolio regarding industry or region concentrations? Are there any asset classes that dominate your portfolio? Why did you choose an abundance of these assets – is it sound reasoning?

_____
_____
_____
_____
_____
_____
_____

Considering your concentrated areas, what risks might your portfolio be exposed to? How might these concentrations impact your portfolio during market fluctuations?

_____
_____
_____
_____
_____
_____
_____

Based on your observations, which industries or regions are underrepresented in your portfolio? What types of asset classes could you consider to achieve a more balanced portfolio? Consider these questions, and reinvent the perfect asset table on the next page, considering how to diversify for security and profitability.

Ideal Diversified Portfolio

Investment Name (Apple, Uber, Etc.)	Asset Class (Bond, Stock, ETF, Etc.)	Industry (Technology, Healthcare, Etc.)	Region (N. America, Europe, Etc.)	Percentage of Your Portfolio

What did you learn about your investment approach from assessing your current portfolio? Were there any surprises or insights regarding your concentration in certain asset classes, industries, or regions?

_____

_____

_____

_____

Chapter 14: You'll Change

Chapter 14 takes an insightful look at how personal finance changes throughout different life phases. Morgan Housel highlights that as we age, our financial priorities and strategies evolve, reflecting our changing circumstances and needs.

In our 20s, the focus is often on establishing a financial foundation. This includes navigating early career choices, managing student debt, and beginning to save and invest for the future. Young adults benefit from the time they have, allowing investments to grow and compound. It's also a period to start thinking about retirement savings, even though it seems far off.

As we move into our 30s and 40s, financial complexities often increase. For many, this is a time of balancing the costs of raising a family and possibly caring for aging parents. It's crucial during these years to avoid the trap of lifestyle inflation, where increased earnings lead to proportionately higher spending. Investments during these years should balance growth and risk management, reflecting the need for both wealth accumulation and stability.

Approaching retirement in the 50s and 60s, the emphasis shifts toward preparing for life post-career. This often means adjusting investment strategies to focus more on wealth preservation and less on aggressive growth. It's a period for fine-tuning retirement plans, paying down debts, and ensuring that the savings will last through the retirement years.

In retirement, the goal shifts to maintaining financial stability and enjoying the fruits of years of saving and investing. This involves managing investments to ensure they provide the necessary income while minimizing risks.

Workbook: The Psychology of Money

Key Points

- Begin financial planning early in your 20s, focusing on debt management and initiating savings.

- In your 30s and 40s, balance family responsibilities with financial growth, and be aware of unnecessary spending increases.

- Transition your financial focus in your 50s and 60s to prepare for retirement, emphasizing wealth preservation.

- During retirement, manage your investments to ensure stability and align your lifestyle with your financial resources.

- Regularly review and adjust your financial plans to accommodate life changes and evolving goals.

Financial Time Capsule

This exercise invites you to set specific financial goals for various life stages, including your 30s, 40s, 50s, and retirement. By doing this, you embark on a process of strategic planning and forward-thinking, which is essential for effective financial management. This exercise is not just about envisioning your future; it's about actively planning and preparing for it.

Identify and document specific financial goals you want to achieve at different life stages (30s, 40s, 50s, retirement). These could include buying a house, saving for children's education, retirement planning, etc.

In my 20s, I'd like to…

In my 30s, I'd like to…

In my 50s, I'd like to…

In my 60s, I'd like to…

Once completed, answer the questions below to reflect on the feasibility and alignment of these goals with your current financial situation and habits.

Having identified your financial goals for each life stage, reflect on what steps you can take now to set the foundation for achieving these objectives. How can your current financial decisions and habits be aligned or adjusted to support these goals?

Chapter 15: Nothing's Free

In Chapter 15, titled "Nothing's Free," the author explores the concept of risk and reward in the context of financial decisions, emphasizing that every financial move carries its own set of risks, even when it seems safest. The chapter begins by debunking the common misconception that there are completely safe investments or financial decisions. It clarifies that while the degree of risk varies, no decision is entirely devoid of risk.

A key theme of the chapter is the inherent trade-off between risk and reward. The author illustrates this through various examples, showing that higher potential rewards are often accompanied by higher risks. This relationship is crucial in understanding investment strategies and financial planning. The chapter explores different types of risks, including market risk, inflation risk, and the risk of not meeting financial goals. It stresses the importance of recognizing and understanding these risks to make informed decisions.

The author also discusses the psychological aspects of risk perception. Often, individuals underestimate or overestimate risks based on past experiences, personal biases, or a lack of understanding. The chapter argues that a balanced view of risk is essential, one that neither magnifies nor minimizes potential threats.

Additionally, the chapter addresses the cost of avoiding risk, particularly the opportunity cost of overly cautious financial strategies. The author argues that while avoiding high-risk investments can protect against losses, it can also lead to missed opportunities for significant growth. This point underscores the need for a well-thought-out balance between risk and potential returns in financial planning.

Key Points

- Every financial decision involves some degree of risk; there are no completely safe investments.

- There is an inherent trade-off between risk and reward in finance, with higher rewards usually accompanied by higher risks.

- Understanding various types of risks, including market risk, inflation risk, and the risk of not meeting financial goals, is crucial.

- Individuals often misjudge risks due to past experiences, biases, or misunderstandings.

- A balanced view of risk, avoiding both underestimation and overestimation, is essential.

- Avoiding risk altogether can lead to missed opportunities for growth, highlighting the importance of balancing risk and potential returns.

- The chapter emphasizes the necessity of managing and balancing risk in pursuit of financial goals.

Opportunity Cost Evaluation

This exercise is designed to help you assess the potential impacts of overly cautious investment strategies. Often, being too risk-averse can lead to missed opportunities for growth, and this exercise aims to make you more aware of these potential costs.

Investment Analysis
List one of your conversative/low risk investments. Look at the recent performance of this investment. How has it grown over the past year or since you invested in it?

Investment	1 Year Growth

Research Alternative Investments
Look into other investment options that carry a slightly higher risk but potentially higher returns. This will take research into fundamentals, performance, and future potential growth. Pick one company/cryptocurrency/concept, then explain why you chose it.

My riskier investment option is _____

I chose this investment option because....

_____
_____
_____
_____

Compare Potential Returns

For your conversative investment, estimate the potential returns over a given period (say 5 or 10 years). Then, do the same for the alternative higher-risk investments. Calculate the different in returns. Use this calculator:

https://www.nerdwallet.com/calculator/investment-calculator

Safe Investment Return	Risky Investment Return	Difference in Returns

Insights from Alternative Investment Research

What did you learn about higher-risk investments during your research? How do the potential rewards and risks of these investments compare to your conservative choices?

_____

_____

_____

Reassessing Investment Strategies

Based on this exercise, do you feel a need to reassess your current investment strategy? What changes, if any, are you considering for your investment approach to balance risk and potential growth? This could be as simple as adding riskier investments to your portfolio, diversifying more, or no change at all.

_____

_____

_____

Chapter 16: You and Me

Chapter 16, titled "You and Me," explores the often overlooked but crucial aspect of personal differences in financial behavior and decision-making. The chapter opens by acknowledging that finance is not one-size-fits-all; what works for one person might not work for another. This idea is central to understanding and respecting the diversity in individual financial strategies and choices.

The chapter explores factors that influence our financial decisions. These include varying levels of wealth, different sources of income, distinct financial goals, and unique personal experiences. The author emphasizes that these differences can lead to vastly different financial behaviors and needs. For example, the risk tolerance of a wealthy individual with multiple income streams might be entirely different from someone relying on a single source of income.

One of the key points discussed is the impact of personal history on financial decisions. The chapter illustrates this with examples of how events like the Great Depression, the dot-com bubble, or the 2008 financial crisis have left lasting impressions on different generations, shaping their attitudes towards saving, investing, and risk.

The author also addresses the psychological aspects, such as how personal fears, biases, and experiences can shape one's approach to money. It's highlighted that understanding these personal dimensions is crucial for both financial advisors and individuals in crafting a financial strategy that is truly aligned with one's unique situation.

This chapter serves as a reminder of the importance of personalization in finance. It argues for a more empathetic and individualized approach to financial planning.

Workbook: The Psychology of Money

Key Points

- Financial strategies are not one-size-fits-all; individual differences significantly impact financial behavior and decisions.

- Key factors influencing financial decisions include levels of wealth, sources of income, financial goals, and personal experiences.

- Wealthier individuals with multiple income streams often have a different risk tolerance compared to those relying on a single income source.

- Personal history, such as experiences with events like the Great Depression, the dot-com bubble, or the 2008 financial crisis, shapes attitudes towards saving, investing, and risk.

- Psychological factors like personal fears, biases, and experiences play a crucial role in shaping an individual's approach to money.

- Understanding these personal dimensions is vital for financial advisors and individuals to create financial strategies that align with unique situations.

- The chapter emphasizes the need for a more empathetic and personalized approach in financial planning, recognizing the diversity in financial needs and strategies.

Identifying Your Financial Fears

The table below will help you systematically assess the validity of each financial fear you have. By breaking down and critically examining each fear, you will be able to differentiate between fears grounded in realistic assessments and those that may be exaggerated by emotional responses or misconceptions. Now, begin by filling out the table below, carefully reviewing each instruction in the columns. Then, answer the reflection questions on the next page.

Financial Fear	Why Do I Have This Fear?	Is It Rational? (Yes/No)	Why or Why Not?
Example: Fear of investment losses	I had a bad experience once.	No	It was only one bad experience – I can learn from it and try again.

Workbook: The Psychology of Money

What patterns, if any, did you notice in your fears? For instance, do your fears predominantly revolve around themes such as the fear of financial loss, anxiety over uncertain economic conditions, or concerns about specific financial decisions?

In instances where you've identified a fear as irrational, what specific strategies can you implement to reshape your perspective on this fear? This could include more education, more risk tolerance, or even just developing a healthier mindset.

If a fear was considered rational, how might you plan to address or mitigate this fear in your financial planning? Consider building a bigger financial safety net, diversifying your portfolio, or setting specific financial goals.

What is your biggest takeaway from this exercise, and how can you implement it into your daily financial life?

Chapter 17: The Seduction of Pessimism

In Chapter 17, titled "The Seduction of Pessimism," the author talks about why being negative often seems smarter and more believable than being positive, especially when it comes to money and investing. The chapter starts off by pointing out that people often think it's wiser or more thoughtful to predict bad things than good things. This kind of negative thinking is really common in finance, where bad news usually gets more attention and seems more trustworthy.

The chapter looks back at the history of financial markets and shows that, even though there have been many tough times and crises, the general direction has been upward. But, people tend to focus more on what could go wrong, which leads to paying too much attention to risks and not enough to how strong and resilient markets can be. The chapter uses examples from past market crashes and economic downturns to show how negative stories can take over, even when there's long-term growth and recovery happening.

A key point in the chapter is about how the media and financial experts often make this negativity worse. They tend to make a big deal out of bad news and focus on the scariest parts of financial information. This can make people see things in a more negative light than they really are. As a result, investors might be too scared or too careful, and they could miss out on good chances to make money.

The author suggests that we need a more balanced way of looking at financial news and analysis. It's important to understand that risks are real and need to be taken seriously, but they shouldn't be the only thing we think about. There's also a chance for good things to happen. The chapter ends by encouraging investors to be aware of how tempting it is to be negative and to try to have a more realistic and balanced view of financial markets.

Workbook: The Psychology of Money

Key Points

- Negative views on finance often seem smarter than positive ones.

- Financial bad news gets more focus and seems more reliable.

- Despite past downturns, financial markets generally grow over time.

- News and experts often highlight the worst parts of financial information.

- This can lead to too much caution in investing, missing good opportunities.

- A balanced view of financial news, considering both risks and positives, is better.

- Investors should understand the appeal of negativity and aim for a realistic view of markets.

Companion Press

Diversifying Your Financial News

Reflect on where you currently get your financial news. Write down the main sources you use. Assess the tone of these sources: Do you find them mostly negative, positive, or neutral? Complete exercise below. Provide specific examples that support your assessment.

My current financial news outlet is negative/positive/neutral. (Circle your answer)

I feel this financial news outlet is this way because…

_____

_____

_____

_____

Research and list other financial news outlets that offer a broader range of perspectives. Some examples of neutral or positive news outlets might include YouTube content, Bloomberg, The Economist, or financial podcasts. Do research and pick your favorite. Which one do you choose to focus on and why?

_____

_____

_____

_____

Remember, never trust just one source. Do your own research and find logical, non-bias, and diversified news sources to develop a well-rounded understanding of financial trends and make informed investment decisions.

Unique Research from UNC

Research from the University of North Carolina experimentally confirms that people learn differently from positive versus negative outcomes, particularly in the context of financial news. The study found that people tend to overreact to bad outcomes or news, leading to overly pessimistic conclusions about future investments. This bias towards pessimism is reflected in the way investors process financial information, often drawing overly pessimistic lessons from negative outcomes or news.

This phenomenon of reacting more pessimistically than warranted, especially in a negative context, is crucial in understanding investment behavior during economic downturns or facing setbacks. It suggests that business leaders and investors might underinvest or be excessively cautious not because of wise caution but due to a hardwired overreaction to bad news. This behavioral pattern can potentially hamper recovery and growth prospects, emphasizing the need for a more balanced approach to interpreting financial news.

You can avoid this by diversifying your information sources. You can look at different types of financial media, such as traditional newspapers, online financial news platforms, and specialized investment journals. It's also beneficial to listen to a range of financial podcasts and watch financial news channels that offer varying perspectives. Additionally, reading reports from different financial analysts and following a mix of market commentators on social media can provide a broader view. This variety in information sources can help counterbalance the negative bias and give a more rounded understanding of the financial markets and investment opportunities.

Chapter 18: When You'll Believe Anything

Chapter 18, titled "When You'll Believe Anything," explores the complexities of financial psychology, particularly how psychological factors contribute to financial bubbles and a tendency towards pessimism in the world of finance. The chapter begins with an examination of significant financial crises, such as the dot-com bubble and the housing crisis, highlighting that these were not solely driven by greed. It posits that a lack of accurate information and critical thinking played a crucial role in these events.

The discussion then shifts to the behavior of investors, particularly how they often follow market trends without considering whether these align with their personal financial goals. This herd mentality, as illustrated by the dot-com bubble, shows how short-term focused trading by day traders can significantly inflate stock prices, creating a disconnect from their long-term value and leading to unstable market conditions.

The chapter places a strong emphasis on the importance of individual investment strategies. It advises readers on the value of understanding their personal financial goals, risk tolerance, and investment time frame, which is essential for maintaining stability despite market ups and downs.

In summary, "When You'll Believe Anything" navigates through the intricacies of financial decision-making, advocating for a well-informed, personalized approach to investing. It encourages readers to consider their unique financial aims and to base their decisions on a comprehensive and balanced understanding of the financial landscape. It encourages a more nuanced understanding of financial markets, advocating for a balance between realism and optimism, and recognizing the powerful role of stories and personal biases in shaping our financial worldviews.

Key Points

- Financial crises like the dot-com and housing bubbles were driven by more than greed; lack of accurate information and critical thinking were key factors.

- Investors often follow market trends without aligning them with personal financial goals, leading to irrational decisions.

- The dot-com bubble exemplified how short-term trading inflated stock prices, disconnecting them from their long-term value.

- Emphasizes the importance of individual investment strategies, considering personal financial goals, risk tolerance, and investment timelines.

- Advocates for a well-informed, personalized approach to investing, balancing realism and optimism.

- Stresses the influence of societal narratives and personal biases in shaping financial decisions and market views.

Companion Press

Herd Mentality in Past Financial Decisions

This exercise is designed to help readers introspectively analyze a past financial decision influenced by herd mentality, as discussed in Chapter 18, "When You'll Believe Anything." It aims to foster a deeper understanding of how following the crowd can impact financial choices.

Recall a specific financial decision you made in the past, where you followed a trend or the actions of other investors. This could be an investment in stocks, cryptocurrencies, real estate, or any other financial market.

_____
_____
_____
_____
_____

Reflect on why you made this decision. Were you influenced by fear of missing out (FOMO), stories of quick gains, or the actions of others in your social or professional circle?

_____
_____
_____
_____
_____

Evaluate the outcome of this decision. Did it align with your long-term financial goals? How did it affect your financial situation and investment portfolio?

_____
_____
_____
_____
_____

Looking back, how do you assess the level of risk you took with this decision? How has this experience shaped your understanding of risk in financial decisions?

_____
_____
_____
_____

Identify the key lessons you learned from this experience. How has this decision influenced your approach to financial decision-making since then? For example, if you invested in a trending stock without proper research and faced a loss, you might have learned the importance of due diligence.

_____
_____
_____
_____
_____

The Bitcoin Bubble Example

In 2017, Bitcoin saw a significant surge in its value, reaching a peak of nearly $20,000 per coin, followed by a sharp decline. This bubble wasn't just driven by the typical greed seen in market speculations; a major contributing factor was the general lack of in-depth understanding of the cryptocurrency market among many investors. Attracted by the allure of quick wealth and driven by a fear of missing out, numerous investors entered the market, often without fully comprehending the underlying technology or considering the potential long-term consequences of their investments.

This situation highlighted a common trend where investors are swayed by market excitement and the promise of high returns, leading them to make decisions that might not align with their long-term financial objectives. The influx into the Bitcoin market was marked by a kind of herd mentality, with many investors jumping on the bandwagon due to the rising hype around cryptocurrencies, rather than based on a rational assessment of the market's future potential.

The events surrounding the Bitcoin bubble in 2017 demonstrate the complexities inherent in financial decision-making. It reflects how societal narratives, speculative excitement, and personal biases can significantly influence financial choices. This episode underlines the necessity of making informed, personalized investment decisions that are based on a thorough understanding of the market dynamics and not merely influenced by prevailing market sentiments or exaggerated news stories.

Chapter 19: All Together Now

Chapter 19, "All Together Now," wraps up the book by bringing together all the main ideas. It talks about how making a financial plan is a personal thing and why it's important to really understand advice about money.

The chapter starts by comparing how doctors used to treat patients a long time ago to how financial advisors work with clients today. In the past, doctors used to make all the decisions for their patients, thinking one solution was good for everyone. But now, doctors focus more on what each patient needs and wants. The chapter says the same idea should apply to financial advice: your money decisions should fit your own goals, what you want, and your situation.

Then, the author shares his own way of handling money. He believes more in being independent than just trying to get rich. This means living within what you can afford, saving a lot, and choosing investments that make you feel secure. He likes using simple, low-cost investment options because they work well for his family's long-term money goals.

The chapter also talks about the mental side of handling money. It says you should manage your money in a way that lets you sleep well at night, not just focus on getting the highest returns or saving a certain amount. The idea is that feeling okay about your finances is just as important as how much money you have.

Lastly, the chapter points out that sometimes what financial experts say to do and what they actually do themselves can be different. This doesn't mean they're being dishonest; it just shows that money decisions can be complex and emotional. The author encourages people to find financial strategies that match their own life and goals, instead of just doing what everyone else says to do.

Companion Press

Key Points

- Financial planning should be personalized, aligning with individual goals, desires, and circumstances

- The evolution from a one-size-fits-all approach in medicine to personalized care mirrors the shift needed in financial advice.

- Personal financial strategies should prioritize independence and living within means over merely accumulating wealth.

- Simple, low-cost investment options can effectively meet long-term financial objectives.

- Financial management should focus on comfort and peace of mind, not just on maximizing returns or adhering to specific saving rates.

- Financial advice can vary; it's important to choose strategies that resonate with one's personal situation and goals, rather than following generic advice.

Workbook: The Psychology of Money

This exercise aims to help you identify the specific elements in your finances that give you a sense of security. By pinpointing these factors, you can better tailor your financial planning to enhance your overall peace of mind.

Write down what aspects of your finances make you feel secure. This could include having a certain amount in savings, being debt-free, owning property, having a steady income, or having insurance coverage.

What Makes You Feel Secure?	Priority (1-6)

Now, assess the gap between where you are, and where you are most secure. For instance, if you rent instead of own, you have a lot of debt, things like that.

Where I'm At	Where I Want to Be

Let's concentrate on your top financial security priority that you haven't yet achieved. Reflecting on the insights and strategies discussed in this book, outline a comprehensive action plan to meet your goal.

Steps to Achieve Your Goal	Timeline
(Example: Begin Researching ETFs.)	*(Example: Giving myself two weeks.)*

Chapter 20: Confessions

Chapter 20, titled "Confessions," is a personal insight from the author into his own financial beliefs and strategies, based on the ideas discussed in "The Psychology of Money." The chapter starts by looking at how the relationship between doctors and their patients has changed over time, especially in making decisions together. This change in medicine is similar to how financial advice has evolved to be more personalized.

The author then talks about his own way of handling money, focusing on being financially independent rather than just rich. He emphasizes living within your means, even if your income goes up, and saving a lot as a way to be financially independent. This choice is about valuing long-term security and freedom more than short-term gains or showing off wealth.

When it comes to investing, the author prefers to keep it simple and thinks long-term. He likes using low-cost index funds because they are less risky than trying to beat the market. This method may not always get the highest returns, but it suits his family's goals and gives them peace of mind.

The chapter ends with the author reminding readers that everyone's financial decisions are unique. He advises finding your own way to manage money that matches your personal goals, needs, and values. The key is to understand that mastering money is a personal journey.

Why a Low Cost Index Fund?

A low-cost index fund is a type of investment that tries to match the performance of a specific part of the stock market, like the S&P 500. It's called "low-cost" because it doesn't cost a lot to manage. Instead of picking and choosing specific stocks, it simply copies what's in the market index it follows.

When you invest in one of these funds, you make money in two main ways: first, if the value of the stocks in the fund goes up, your shares in the fund become more valuable. Second, you can earn money from dividends, which are small payments made to you from the profits of the companies in the fund.

One of the big benefits of these funds is that they spread out your investment over many different stocks. This means your risk is lower compared to investing in just one or a few stocks. They're generally a good choice for long-term investing because they tend to grow steadily over time.

However, like all investments, there are risks. If the stock market goes down, the value of your index fund will also go down. But because these funds are easy to understand and have a history of good performance, they are often recommended for people who want a simpler way to invest in the stock market.

Key Points

- Highlights the shift in financial advice towards personalization, similar to changes in doctor-patient relationships.

- Emphasizes financial independence and living within one's means as key to the author's financial approach.

- Advocates for simple, long-term investment strategies, with a preference for low-cost index funds due to their lower risk and suitability for his family's goals.

- Stresses the uniqueness of financial decisions, encouraging readers to find strategies that align with their personal goals and values.

Choosing a Low Cost Index Fund

Research 5 different low-cost index funds available in the market. Note down their expense ratios, the index they track, their historical performance, potential pros, and potential cons. (Note: a ratio less than 2% is often considered good. Some of the most cost-effective index funds are as low as .03% to .05%.)

Fund/Index	Expense Ratio	Performance	Pros	Cons

Based on your research and comparison of different low-cost index funds, select the one that best aligns with your investment goals and risk tolerance.

Why did you choose this index fund? What made it stick out compared to the others? For example, this can be because of its expense ratio, historical performance, risk/return profile, diversification with your current portfolio, or personal knowledge about the focus of this index fund.

Companion Press

Thank you!

Greetings from Companion Press, a dedicated team of students, writers, editors, designers, and researchers passionate about creating enriching companion workbooks. Our mission is to enhance your reading experience by offering insightful, practical, and engaging workbooks that complement your favorite best-sellers.

We are deeply grateful for your support, which fuels our passion and enables us to continue doing what we love. It's our sincere hope that this workbook has provided you with valuable insights and practical tools that you can integrate into your daily life, enriching your personal and spiritual journey.

Your feedback means the world to us. If you found this workbook helpful and enjoyable, we kindly ask you to consider leaving us a five-star review on Amazon. Your positive reviews not only motivate us but also help others discover our workbooks, allowing us to expand our reach and continue producing high-quality content.

Thank you once again for being a part of our journey. Your support helps us grow and continue to create workbooks that make a difference in people's lives. We look forward to bringing you more engaging and transformative companion workbooks in the future.

The Companion Press Team

Made in United States
Troutdale, OR
11/17/2024

24946169R00055